FIORE

By

Sharon Felicia Acheampong,

Kaede Nakagawa &

Alton Mazvarirwofa Jr.

First Printing: 2019

ISBN : 978-0-359-66578-5

Yamagata-shi, Yamagata-ken 990-0829

Japan

FIORE

By

Sharon Felicia Acheampong,

Kaede Nakagawa &

Alton Mazvarirwofa Jr.

CONTENTS

FOREWORD

Inspiration is all around us. All it takes is us opening our eyes and recognising it as inspiration for expression. All poems contained in this collection carry a reference to different flowers whether it be what they are said to symbolise or how the poet perceives them. It is not just beauty, each petal, stem leaf, bulb has a story to tell….only if we are willing to listen.

Below is a list of the flowers in order of their relevant poems.

- Dandelion
- Lace Leaf
- Red Rose
- Statice
- Lily
- Chrysanthemum
- Sunflower
- King Protea
- Carnation
- Birds of Paradise
- Aster
- Alstroemeria
- Lilac
- Queen Anne's Lace
- Sword Lily
- Gladiolus
- Ranunculus

SFA

ALTON MAZVARIRWOFA JR.

THE BEE AND THE DANDELION

There was once a chipper bee,

Let's for the meantime call him Fred,

For he was the loner of the swarm,

So stubborn and hard in the head.

Everyday Fred searched through the land,

Looking for the perfect flower.

One day, while flying high above a rose field,

He flew into a dandelion that towered.

Intrigued by how different this dandelion was,

To its neighbouring flora,

He visited it daily,

And found out her name was Donna.

Fred liked spending his afternoons with Donna,

And she adored his company also.

For in their separate worlds they were considered outcasts,

And because of this, they were drawn to each other.

And though Fred and Donna knew,

That they were an odd pair,

They fell in love almost instantly,

As if it was some part of a cruel dare.

Donna poured out her heart to Fred,
About the hardships she faced in the life she led,
Because she was different from the rest.
But that difference,
Is what made Fred adore her even more.
For Fred knew what it was like to have hardships,
To be the outcast of the group,
He related to Donna in every way,
And constantly thought to himself,
"She is just like me"

And Donna had three seedlings,
Growing at the root of her stem,
Which she protected and loved quite dearly,
Like a queen with her favourite gems.
One bad day, so unexpectedly,
Fred was excitedly flying to go see Donna,
Only to realise she was not there anymore,
She had been taken indoors to become a pot flower.
She had been transplanted with her beloved seedlings,
So there was a silver lining,

But he couldn’t be with her again,

But it did not stop him from trying.

But one day, after a while,

He saw her through a window,

And knew something was wrong.

For some reason, she had been robbed of her cheer.

He looked at the bottom of her stem,

And could only see two of her seedling kin.

But upon a brisk search for the third one,

He realised it had wilted into the wind.

Seeing how heartbroken Donna was,

He couldn’t help but feel guilty.

For she needed someone and he wasn’t there,

If only he had looked for her with more urgency,

She thought he didn’t care about her seedlings,

Because they were not attached to him,

As they were to her.

But he could not get close enough to explain,

That he also loved them,

Because he loved Donna.

KAEDE NAKAGAWA

ANTHURIUMS PROMISE

Just so you know,

I will always be here.

I might not be what you want,

But I can be what you need.

A hug, a touch, a shoulder, a hand.

I'd say the door is open,

But there is no door,

You can come and go as you please.

My roots run deep,

So I am not going anywhere.

My heart, my arms, forever open wide.

I just want to see you happy,

Just to see you smile,

Just to know that for a while,

You felt better because of me.

If there is ever anything more,

You just let me know,

For you nothing is ever too much.

For you no mountain is too high,

For you anything, I will do.

ROSA

I will love you till forever,

Till the world sees its end,

And goes down in flames,

Or is it up in smoke?

I will love you for always, in rain or shine

And whatever else is in between.

I will love you when I laugh,

I will love you when I cry.

I will love you through my pleasure,

I will love you through my pain.

You might see it, you might not.

You might feel it, or choose not to.

I will still love you,

Be it in darkness or in light.

For this is not me putting on a show,

Waiting for stage direction,

Lights! Camera! Action!

This is me living out my purpose,

And even when you break my heart,

I will still love you, with all its tiny pieces.

REMEMBER ME STATICE

This is for the day we met,

Paths crossed by chance,

It could have been anyone else, but fate chose us.

This is for the day we realised,

How we were actually meant to be,

And not just two beings,

Thrown together for conveniences sake.

This is for our first fight,

Oh so dramatic, oh so vocal.

Even a volcanic eruption pales in comparison.

This is for the first make-up,

So cute, so sincere.

Were it not for the scars,

It just might have been,

Like it never happened in the first place.

This is for all our memories,

The good ones and the bad ones,

The laughs and the tears.

All secure in my heart,

Never to be forgotten.

QUEEN LILY

My queen, my love, there is none like you,

My queen, your majesty,

There is none else to rule my heart.

For this kingdom is yours,

In all its fullness,

In all its entirety,

Holding back nothing,

Baring it all for you.

No lies, no secrets.

No hidden agendas,

No veiled intentions.

You hold its existence,

In the palm of your hand, yes you do.

Caress or crush it,

Do as you will,

For you answer to no-one,

You are the end all and be-all.

Your decisions I accept,

Be they to bring me pleasure or pain.

For I am but a willing servant, here to serve you at all cost.

CHRYS

Do you trust me?

Please say you do.

I might hurt you,

But it is only for your good.

For how can you know pleasure?

If you have never experienced pain?

Isn't it after all,

A game of comparisons?

In and out, up and down,

Happy and sad, good and evil.

I will never give you,

More than you can handle.

You are much stronger,

Than you realise.

I see you clearer, than you perceive yourself.

Give me your hand,

And do not let go of mine.

I promise you roses, but they come with thorns.

I promise you rain, but it shall always,

Be laced with rainbows at the end.

SHARON FELICIA ACHEAMPONG

SUNS AND FLOWERS

I raise my face to the sky,

I feel the sun on my skin; its rays caress me,

So gently, so lovingly,

It can do me no harm.

I feel myself unravel,

All the tension that's been,

Oh so tightly wound up,

Slowly coming undone.

Being warmed up,

From the outside right to the core.

I feel my wings start to spread,

Could it really be happening?

Am I really going to fly again?

I look around and see them,

Beautiful, all spread out like that.

Held up by a gentle breeze,

Turned into a glistening spectacle,

By the sun's rays.

I feel the joy well up inside, I am happy, I am loved.

All is right with my world.

SELF CROWNED KING

Why not, indeed why not?

Why is on everyone else's lips,

Why I can't, they can't or maybe won't.

Why it's so, it isn't or maybe excuses.

But I sing a different tune,

Not because I am stubborn or rebellious you see,

I just never got the memo,

That had the right notes.

They call it a curse, glad I am not they.

How they look at my differences,

And shake their heads in pity.

I am not beautiful, why not?

I cannot be successful, why not?

I do not deserve love, why not?

I cannot achieve my dreams, why not?

I mean why not me?

I am different, so what?

I will do it, so get out of my way,

I shall succeed, so stand back and enjoy the show.

PRIDE BEAUTY AND NATIONS

Mirror mirror on the wall,

Who's the fairest of them all?

I love it when I hear you say,

My name and fairest all in one line.

They say it's only a matter of time,

And in that time you will say a different name.

But really, why worry about then?

When now is so good?

Belle of the ball,

Star of the show,

I carry the spotlight in my being.

Walk into a room,

Everything comes to a halt,

All eyes, thoughts on me.

They wouldn't dare be anywhere else.

Maybe I should tone it down,

Just a tiny bit. But how do I make myself,

Any less spectacular, I was born this way!

It's not like I chose it, I just nurture it.

Fate dealt me this hand.

HEAVEN ON WINGS

It was a little packet,

Pretty insignificant you see,

Not even that expensive.

But that is a matter of opinion you know.

The label said joy-joys,

Whatever that was supposed to mean.

The instructions were on the back,

Of course, where else would they be?

They were pretty straightforward,

1, 2 and three.

Plant them in your heart, as many as you wish.

Water them with love patience and kindness,

Often for best results.

Nurture and prune them when they sprout,

And allow yourself to see,

The beauty and joy,

Which your heart can create if you let it be.

Do not stifle the laughter,

Do not muffle the song,

For there is beauty even in an off-key tone.

ASTERS GIFT

Good things, that is such a broad term,

Humans should really work,

On the art of simplicity,

Decomplexifying everything.

Sometimes it is just too much work,

Trying to figure out the question.

Leaves no energy to tackle the answer.

Back to my issue,

See, complexities make for easy diversions.

Anyway, good things.

For me, it is only a good thing.

And that is you.

I don't know you,

No idea where or who you are,

But I know you are out there,

And our paths shall collide,

As destiny has set them to.

And until then, I shall wait.

For patience is a virtue,

And good things come to those who wait.

BFF'S

I love never agreeing with you,

Sometimes I do it on purpose.

Just to bug you,

Then I can giggle about it later.

You really are so cute,

When you are trying to prove a point,

Show me a certain way, normally the right way,

Not that I will admit it then.

Your mind is brilliant,

It is an honour to watch it work.

I love sitting in silence with you,

Not because we have nothing to say,

But because our hearts can speak,

When our lips do not utter a word.

I love having you on speed-dial,

And knowing you will always pickup

Whether I am in trouble or I just miss you.

You are always there to listen.

I love having you as my friend,

Had I had been given a choice, I would still have chosen you

WILTED YOUTH

The gentle movement of the swings,

Up and down, up and down,

The ups not way up, the downs not way down.

Everything is just right.

All perfect, all in place.

Never too little never too much.

The merry go round,

Going round and round in circles

When you start and when you stop,

Everything is still there,

Even though it is moving a bit.

But it is just as it should be.

All is right with the world.

The see-saw rise and falls,

A perfect balance, you are either up or down,

No in be tweens, no grey areas.

It's black or its white, its yes or its no.

That is how the world should be.

Or should have stayed,

Because I grew up and everything changed.

ROYAL PRISON

Down here it is just me,

And that is perfectly fine.

I wouldn’t want it any other way.

Down here, there are no surprises,

No sudden turn of events, or unexpected surprises.

I know me and I know me,

There is no-one else just me.

Down here all by myself I am safe, they say alone.

They do not understand, no not at all.

That it’s them who broke me,

Them who hurt and haunt me,

Them who taunt and torture me,

Them that drive me to these depths.

Not that I complain, they can’t follow me here.

For here is a place,

One place in the whole wide world,

That I can call my own,

My safe place, my comfort zone,

My sanctuary.

REBORN

In my next life, next because this one is done,

I want to be you, or just like you.

With loyalty oozing from your every pore.

And grace in each step you take.

Determination etched on your face,

Translating into everything you do.

Clarity in your thoughts,

That helps you persevere against all odds.

Reaching for dreams,

They said you could not dream,

Soaring in skies

They said you would not fly in.

And all around you, a halo of love.

You give so much of it,

And get even more in return.

In my next life I want to be you,

Because I have made such a mess of this one,

I need some form of redemption

RADIANT

You were bright,

So bright I was blinded.

I wanted to look at you,

So that I would remember you.

But every time I opened my eyes,

All I saw was light

.It took me a while to figure out,

Forgive me for being slow.

But that is what you were,

Are and continue to be.

Light and more light,

Illuminating my life,

My heart and my soul.

Chasing the darkness away, melting the cobwebs too.

Reawakening me from my slumber,

That despair induced sleep.

Stay, don't go. You are light, you are radiant.

You show me the way; I do not stumble so much.

You give me warmth, you give me love.

www.ingramcontent.com/pod-product-compliance
Ingram Content Group UK Ltd.
Pitfield, Milton Keynes, MK11 3LW, UK
UKHW041901190726
13854UKWH00003B/1016

9 780359 665785